ELEPHANT AND BAZU'S

DARING ESCAPE

Steven Otfinoski

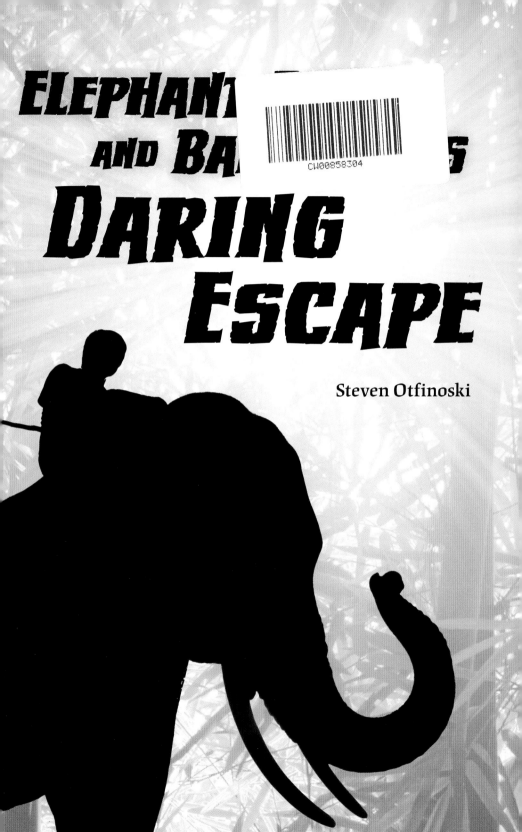

raintree

a Capstone company — publishers for children

Engage Literacy is published in the UK by Raintree.
Raintree is an imprint of Capstone Global Library Limited, a company incorporated in England and Wales
having its registered office at 264 Banbury Road, Oxford, OX2 7DY – Registered company number:
6695582

www.raintree.co.uk

Editorial credits
Jennifer Huston, Clare Lewis and Alesha Sullivan editors; Kazuko Collins and Charmaine Whitman,
designers; Svetlana Zhurkin, media researcher; Steve Walker, production specialist

Image credits
Alamy: Morten Svenningsen, 31, PC Jones Travel, 53; AP Photo, 19; Bridgeman Images: Look and Learn/
Private Collection/Illustration from "Elephant Bill" (color litho), Salinas, Alberto (1932–2004), 12, 23,
27, 37, 42, 47, 55, Look and Learn/Private Collection/The elephant trek of Elephant Bill (gouache on
paper), English School (20th century), 41, Penlee House Gallery and Museum, Penzance, Cornwall, UK/
Elephant Bill, 1956 (oil on canvas), Bruford, Marjorie Frances (1903–1958), 58; Getty Images: Keystone,
cover (bottom), Popperfoto, 6; iStockphoto: lim_jessica, 29; Library of Congress, back cover, 5 (bottom);
Newscom: Heritage Images/The Print Collector, 9, 21, imageBROKER/Michael Runkel, 50–51, Mirrorpix/
Indian Official Photograph, 15, Pictures From History, 17, Zuma Press/David Woodfal, 61; Shutterstock:
apiguide, cover (left), 1 (front), Ivsanmas, 5 (top), Sam DCruz, 25, szefei (bamboo forest), cover
(background) and throughout, worradirek, 4, 14, 18, 24, 28, 36, 40, 46, 52, 56, 60; Svetlana Zhurkin, 57

21 20 19 18 17
10 9 8 7 6 5 4 3 2 1
Printed and bound in China.

Elephant Bill and Bandoola's Daring Escape

ISBN: 978 1 4747 4588 8

CONTENTS

A bond renewed 4

Elephant Bill 14

Operation evacuation 18

Bandoola leads the way 24

Mission impossible 28

A staircase of stone 36

A dangerous ascent 40

The march to freedom 46

The war winds down 52

The end of a friendship 56

Elephants at work today 60

Timeline 62

Glossary 63

Index 64

A BOND RENEWED

James Howard Williams, better known as "Elephant Bill", took a deep breath of the hot, humid air. It felt good to be back in Burma. He'd been in India for a while, serving the British Army during World War II (1939–1945). But now he was back and ready to *recruit*, or seek someone out, for his bridge-building Elephant Company. He looked around the thick forest of *teak* trees and the mountains that lay beyond it. Williams had been a teak logging boss here for about 20 years. He loved the work, the land and the workers – including a group of elephants that he trained to haul logs to the mills.

Williams had always loved animals. As a child back in Cornwall, his first pet was a donkey called Prince. Later he had a camel called Frying Pan and several dogs. While serving in World War I (1914–1918), he worked with camels and mules that carried war supplies.

India Burma

Elephants were used in
Burma to haul logs.

Japanese soldiers invaded Burma in 1941.

After World War I ended, Williams was recruited by the Bombay Burma Trading Corporation. It was a company that collected tea, teak and other goods. That's when he moved to Burma and began working with elephants.

Williams came to love elephants above all other animals. They were his colleagues, his friends and his second family. He even knew a thousand elephants by name.

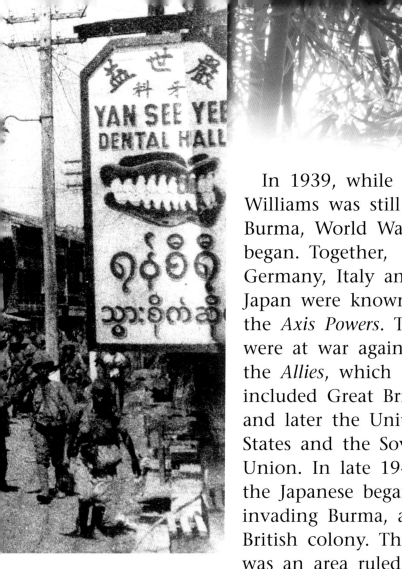

In 1939, while Williams was still in Burma, World War II began. Together, Germany, Italy and Japan were known as the *Axis Powers*. They were at war against the *Allies*, which included Great Britain and later the United States and the Soviet Union. In late 1941, the Japanese began invading Burma, a British colony. This was an area ruled by the British in south-eastern Asia. Within months, the Japanese had taken control of most of the country. That's when Williams and other employees of the Bombay Burma Trading Corporation and their families had to leave Burma. For safety, they fled to nearby India, a colony still in British hands. Williams was forced to leave behind his much loved elephants. For how long, he didn't know.

While in India, Williams was given a job with the British Army. Because he knew almost every jungle road, river and piece of *terrain* in Burma, he was given a job in the Intelligence Branch. In this role, Williams provided important information to help the British forces plan their struggle against the Japanese.

However, Williams wanted to get back to his elephants in Burma and play a more active role in the war. He explained to his bosses that elephants could carry supplies and build bridges for the troops. Williams told them that these "elephant bridges" would be simple and could be built quickly. The elephants would haul logs into place and push them tightly together to form a bridge.

After Williams convinced his bosses to let him return to Burma and his elephants, he headed back to the *remote* teak forest he knew so well. On the way, he decided who he would recruit for his company. Of course, he would need expert elephant handlers or *mahouts*. He would also need a few experienced Army men like himself, who knew and respected the Burmese culture.

His friend Harold Browne immediately came to mind. Williams later recalled that Browne was more loved by the Burmans than anyone else he worked with. Browne knew lots about elephants, too. Williams also recruited Stanley White. He said of Browne and White that their knowledge of the Burmese people was very useful.

As Williams' group was slowly coming together, he put out the word that he needed elephants and their handlers. His top choice was a master mahout called Po Toke and his elephant, Bandoola.

> "*Bandoola was ... 'the tubbiest little male elephant calf ever born'.*"
>
> –JH Williams, *Bandoola*

Of all the elephants Williams had ever worked with, Bandoola was his favourite. They had been friends for more than 20 years and had even been born in the same month of the same year. Williams first met Bandoola at a logging camp early in his career in Burma. Bandoola was already well known and was under the care of Po Toke, who had reared him from a chubby calf. The first time Williams ran his hand over Bandoola's thick trunk, he immediately felt a special bond with the animal. He said he had "a feeling of understanding him as a fellow-creature closer than many human beings".

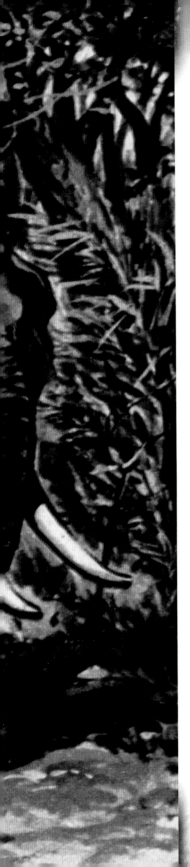

Bandoola stood over 2.7 metres tall, with greyish skin, dots of pink freckles on his chest and a pair of long curved tusks. Williams was relieved to be reunited with him. There was no other elephant he had more faith in. With Bandoola on his team, he knew without a doubt that his company would be a success.

Bandoola poked Williams with his trunk. Williams rubbed his thick skin and whispered in his large ear. He told Bandoola that they had a very important mission. He was going to be enrolled as Number 1 War Elephant. He would be the first of the elephants to fight for the freedom of Burma.

ELEPHANT BILL

Williams' company quickly took shape. With Po Toke's help, more and more mahouts joined up and brought their elephants with them. In a short time, Williams' group grew from one elephant to more than 1,600.

Williams moved his main office to the village of Moreh near the border of Burma and India. Bandoola was part of a special group of about 45 elephants working a few kilometres away. On 2 December 1942, Williams' elephants began work on the first bridge. They would build hundreds more bridges over the next year.

All was going well with the Elephant Company until one day in March 1944 when Williams received a call to report to the boss's office. "This is Top Secret," the boss said. Williams' heart skipped a couple of beats. He braced himself for what his boss was about to say.

Williams' boss told him the Japanese would be moving into the area soon and the Allies would be planning a counter-attack. The Elephant Company would be in danger. So Williams would have to move the group to safety while the fighting took place. They would go to India, which was still protected by the Allies.

Williams' boss asked how long it would take to round up all the elephants and start moving out. Williams thought for a moment. He didn't want to leave, but he knew he didn't have a choice. Orders were orders. Williams told his boss that he could be ready to move out in five days. The boss ordered him to start organizing the *evacuation* straight away.

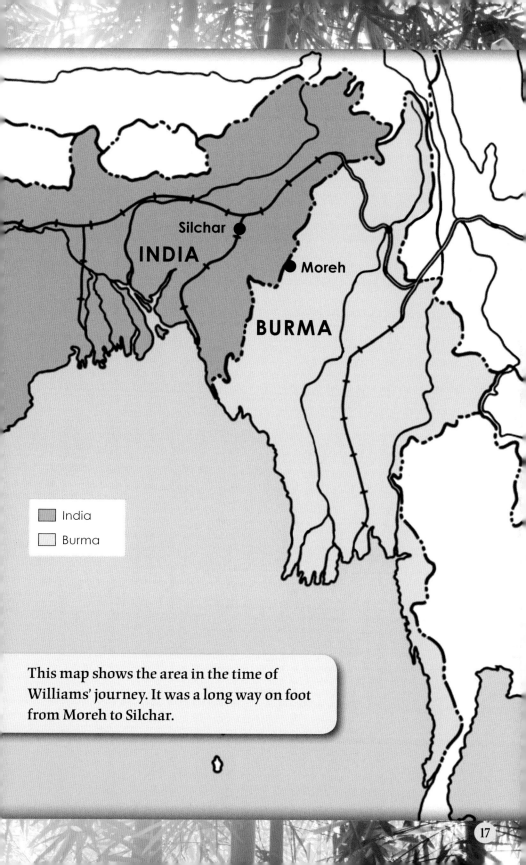

Silchar

INDIA

Moreh

BURMA

India
Burma

This map shows the area in the time of
Williams' journey. It was a long way on foot
from Moreh to Silchar.

OPERATION EVACUATION

Williams knew the journey from Burma into India would be a difficult one. The Japanese controlled most of the roads out of the country. This meant Williams' group would have to travel on jungle paths and through the mountains. It was over 190 kilometres to their journey's end – a British tea *plantation* in Silchar. This town was in the Indian state of Assam. They would have to cross a total of five mountain ranges with peaks reaching 1,500 to 1,800 metres high. British officers told Williams it would be better if he left the elephants behind. But he knew what would happen if he did. The animals would probably be injured or killed during the fighting.

As Williams formed the company for escape, the group grew to more than 130 mahouts and soldiers and 53 elephants. There were 45 adults and 8 calves. Williams divided the company into smaller groups to make the trip easier. Bandoola, of course, would lead them.

Elephants like this one were loaded with food and supplies for the journey.

Then, just as Williams was getting ready for the *trek*, a group of 69 weary, unwell and half-starved women and children arrived at the camp. Some of the women were pregnant; others were old and frail. Williams felt full of sympathy for them.

They were *refugees* from Nepal. They were women and children whose husbands and fathers were *Gurkha* soldiers fighting the Japanese. They were also trying to get to safety in India.

Williams knew that without skilled soldiers leading them, the chances of the refugees surviving the journey were slim. On the other hand, he knew that if he agreed to take them, it would slow down his group and risk their lives.

The Nepalese refugees were the wives and children of Gurkha soldiers.

In the end, Williams decided to take the refugees with him. There were some among his group who disagreed with his choice. But they accepted his decision.

Williams knew he would need plenty of luck. Five of the refugees – the pregnant women and some of the elderly – left on a small aeroplane. That left 64 women and children, plus Williams' men. Williams had enough food *rations* loaded onto the elephants to last them for 15 days. He hoped that they would arrive at the plantation before their food ran out.

At dawn on 5 April 1944, the company moved out. More than 200 people and 53 elephants headed out on a dangerous journey into the unknown.

BANDOOLA LEADS THE WAY

For eight days – from dawn to dusk – the group trudged through the jungle and over mountain peaks. The days were hot and the nights were often cold and rainy. Some of the women and children became ill and had to be cared for. Food rations were limited and many members of the group grew weak from lack of food. Insects bit them a lot as they walked. They often heard gunfire in the distance. It was a grim reminder that the fighting was close by. Despite everything, no one complained. The women who were strong enough used jungle knives to cut through the thick bamboo and *vegetation* to create a path wide enough for the elephants.

As they climbed higher and higher, some of the elephants, often the older ones, became tired and slowed down. But not Bandoola. He led with strength and courage. He was, in Elephant Bill's words, "the pride of the forest".

The Burmese jungles were thick and difficult to cross.

On the ninth day, Williams decided to set out ahead of the others to inspect the terrain. He soon found himself in a remote area with a creek and *lush*, green plants and grass. He decided that it would be the perfect spot to rest. There was plenty of water for everyone to drink and plants and grass for the elephants to eat.

Williams crossed the creek and went on for about three more kilometres. Then he saw it – a cliff face rising over 90 metres into the sky. His heart sank, but he didn't lose hope. There had to be an opening in the rock that they could pass through. He followed the sandstone cliff for another kilometre or so, but he still couldn't find one. The very large cliff would be impossible to cross. Williams doubted anyone could climb it safely, and the elephants surely could not. It looked like that officer had been right. Perhaps Elephant Bill had been wrong to think he could lead his elephants to safety. It looked as though they had reached the end of the line.

MISSION IMPOSSIBLE

While Williams waited for the others, he tried to come up with a plan. While some people may have thought it was impossible to climb the enormous cliff – even for a mountain goat – Elephant Bill had an idea. He noticed that the sandstone had been *eroded* by weather and time. Nature had made many jagged *outcroppings* in the cliff, forming crude footholds, or steps, in the rock. Williams realized that it might be possible to use these cracks in the rock as steps.

When the group caught up with him, Williams explained the problem. Everyone stared in silence at the towering cliff face. He told them that they'd camp there for a few days and work out a solution. The women cheered at the thought of a few days of rest. But rest was not part of Williams' plan.

Cliffs in Burma can rise steeply out of the jungle.

At dawn the next day, officer Browne started climbing the cliff face where the footholds were. And officers White and CW Hann explored the north and south ends of the cliff. As the group looked on with concern, Browne slowly made his way up the cliff face, climbing from foothold to foothold. When he finally reached the top, the men breathed a sigh of relief. Then Browne slowly made his way down again.

Williams was relieved that Browne had proven that climbing the cliff was possible. White and Hann were not able to climb the cliff. The next morning, Elephant Bill, Po Toke, Browne and several others went back to climb the cliff just as Browne had done.

It was a difficult decision for Elephant Bill because he was afraid of heights. But he thought that if he could get up the cliff, despite his fears, then the rest of the group should be able to as well.

Today's climbers use modern equipment to help them climb cliffs. Browne's attempt was more dangerous.

Williams took a deep breath and began his *ascent*. As he climbed higher, he focused his eyes upwards for fear of looking down. He knew if he did look down, he might panic and fall. He crawled much of the way on his hands and knees.

> "I preferred to crawl a good part of the way on all fours!"
>
> –JH Williams, *Elephant Bill*

As he approached the top, his foot slipped on the rocks. He grabbed onto the step above him with his sweaty hands and held on for dear life. His head began to spin. He regained his footing, took a brief rest and kept climbing upwards. After what seemed like forever, he finally made it to the top. He was out of breath but proud of what he had achieved. As he came back down, his heart pounded in his chest with every step. He had made it, but how would the women and children ever make it up the cliff? And what about the elephants?

When he was finally on solid ground again, Williams had an idea. He told the group that nature had made those footholds. He explained that they could make more of them. Williams thought that if the sandstone was soft enough, they could cut into it with their knives. They could carve out more steps until they'd made something like a staircase that everyone could climb. Williams told the others that if they made the steps wide enough, even the elephants could climb them. But he secretly wondered if that would be possible, given the animals' size.

The other men slowly nodded their heads. They were willing to give Elephant Bill's idea a go. What other choice did they have? If they turned back, they'd be captured by the enemy soldiers. They had no choice but to give it a go.

"In some places [the cliff] was so steep that the elephants would almost be standing on their hind legs."

–JH Williams, *Elephant Bill*

A STAIRCASE OF STONE

The next morning, the group began hacking away at the cliff face. Men and women cut away the thick plants, grasses and sandstone with jungle knives. Men from local villages came to help.

By the end of the day, they had carved out what looked like a crude set of steps to the top of the cliff. Williams decided he would test the staircase himself. This time he felt less fearful. The path was wider, and the plants and grasses that had been cut were stacked up along the edge of the cliff, blocking his view down below. Williams was rather impressed with the amount of work they'd completed in just one day. Even so, he still had doubts about making the path and steps wide enough for the elephants. But he also knew they had no other choice but to keep going.

The next morning, they went back to work on the steps so the elephants could get up them. As night fell they surveyed their work. The staircase was wide enough for the elephants, but only just in some spots. And they couldn't afford to spend one more day working on the steps. They knew the Japanese might appear at any moment.

Williams went over to check the elephants. They appeared calm, peaceful and unaware of the terrible challenge that lay ahead. But Williams couldn't stop the dark thoughts going through his head. If just one elephant were to slip, it would fall on the others, and they would go down like dominoes. It would be a disaster.

Elephant Bill expressed his concerns to Po Toke. "All will be well," Po Toke said quietly with a smile. "Bandoola will lead and if he won't face it no other elephant will."

Williams took some comfort from his old friend's words. If he had faith in anyone in the group, it was Bandoola. If anyone could meet the challenge and lead the other elephants up the cliff, it was him.

> **"Bandoola will lead and if he won't face it no other elephant will."**
>
> —Po Toke, *Elephant Bill*

A DANGEROUS ASCENT

Early the next morning, they set out on their dangerous mission. Bandoola led the elephants, followed by the rest of the group. Elephant Bill started the climb first. Up the stone staircase he scrambled. It was easier than the last time. The chill of fear he once felt had nearly gone, but he still didn't dare look down.

When he was halfway up the cliff, Williams stopped and turned to look down into the valley. He sat on the sandstone steps and waited for Bandoola and Po Toke.

An hour passed and then another. Still there was no sight of Bandoola coming up the cliff. Had he got up part way and then turned around, afraid to go on? Or even worse, was Bandoola stuck on the steps, frightened and unable to move forwards or backwards?

"I could hear nothing but the burble of the waters of the creek rushing over its boulders far below, and ... the distant thuds of gunfire coming from ... the south."

–JH Williams, *Elephant Bill*

Williams couldn't stand the dark thoughts running through his head, and he was becoming anxious waiting for Po Toke and Bandoola to appear. Just then he heard the sound of heavy footfalls on stone. There, coming into the sunlight below, he saw a giant elephant head and the curved tusks he knew. It was Bandoola!

"Bandoola's head and tusks suddenly came round the corner below me," Williams later recalled. "He looked almost as though he were standing on his hind legs. Then up came his hindquarters as though in a slow-motion picture." Po Toke was with him. He didn't say a word. He just gave Elephant Bill an encouraging look.

Elephant Bill ran to meet Bandoola and rubbed his trunk, but he said nothing. He knew the huge effort it took Bandoola to get up the cliff, and he didn't want to distract him with words. Instead, he waved to Po Toke and turned to continue up the cliff face, knowing Bandoola would follow.

When Williams reached the top, he sat and waited once more. Again, two hours passed, but this time he wasn't worried. When he finally saw Bandoola trudging towards him, Williams felt a rush of joy. Behind Bandoola, the other elephants soon appeared. They had all made it to the top of the cliff. But some of them were so nervous that their legs shook wildly. The soldiers and refugees were right behind them.

It was a long, difficult process getting all the elephants to the top of the cliff. It was night-time when the last member of the company made it to the top.

> *"I learned more in that one day about what elephants could do than I had in twenty-four years. It was a moment of greatness ..."*
>
> –JH Williams, *Elephant Bill*

THE MARCH TO FREEDOM

The Elephant Company had overcome a rather large problem, but other challenges lay ahead. They spent the night on the ridge of the cliff and then climbed down the other side at dawn. The journey down was almost as steep but less rugged. At the bottom of the cliff, they came to a river. Both the humans and elephants rested and drank their fill of water. From there, they began following the winding river. Elephant Bill knew from his map that it would take them to the tea plantation in Silchar.

But the land they crossed was full of danger. They waded through swamps, circled around pools of quicksand and slashed their way through thick forests. They were also in grave danger of running out of food. The children and women were given larger portions of the shrinking rations. And the soldiers got only small servings. The women made flatbread and the soldiers hunted and killed wild animals along the way. However, they still did not have enough food.

Tired and weak from a lack of food, the group's pace slowed. On one day they covered only 16 kilometres in 12 hours. As they got closer to the tea plantation, Elephant Bill decided that a small group would get there faster. He also felt it was best not to alarm the plantation workers. They might mistake a large group for a force of attacking Japanese soldiers. So the next morning, Elephant Bill went on ahead with just nine elephants and their mahouts. The sickest and weakest children rode atop the elephants. Bandoola alone had eight children on his enormous back. The rest of the group stayed behind and waited for the others to bring help.

Anxious to reach the plantation, Elephant Bill ventured ahead of the small group. Soon he found himself enclosed by green tea, as far as he could see. He could hardly believe his eyes and felt very moved by the sight. As he trudged onwards he came to a house. A man in a white shirt was sitting on the front porch. He rose to his feet when he saw Elephant Bill.

It took Williams a moment or two to understand what the man was saying. The man talked to him in a strong Scottish accent. He said, "Where are you coming from and where are you going to?"

Williams told him he was coming from Burma and going to Assam. It was 26 April 1944. After three weeks, their long journey was finally over.

A tea plantation

THE WAR WINDS DOWN

The man who greeted Elephant Bill was James Sinclair, the person who ran the plantation. He invited Williams to join him for breakfast. The coffee and fresh eggs was the best meal Elephant Bill had eaten since leaving Burma.

Soon Bandoola and the other elephants arrived. Sinclair made plans for the sick children to be seen by the local doctor. Williams also contacted a commanding group in Silchar. They rescued the remaining women and children and moved them to a refugee camp. The rest of the group relaxed at the plantation as Sinclair's guests.

Elephant Bill was anxious to see his wife and children in Assam. But all the stress he'd been under resulted in a stomach *ulcer*. He had to be treated in hospital for this sore. It took six weeks for the ulcer to heal. By then Williams couldn't wait to get back to his elephants.

An old-style tea plantation bungalow in Assam

When Williams returned to Silchar, he found Bandoola and the other elephants well rested and ready to go to work. Their part of Burma was once again safe. So they were able to return and build more bridges for the Allies. By December 1944 they had built 270 bridges.

By the end of 1944, the Japanese were moving out of Burma. The war carried on, but it would soon be over. Elephant Bill felt both happy and a little sad. On the one hand, he knew his company had played a key role in defeating the enemy. Yet he knew once the war was over, he would return to England with his family after many years spent in Burma. Bandoola and the other elephants would have to stay behind. It made Williams sad to think that it would soon be time to leave because he knew how much he would miss his favourite elephant.

THE END OF A FRIENDSHIP

One day in late 1944, Williams came to visit Bandoola at his work camp and was told that he was missing. Williams sent a search party to look for him. The party soon returned with sad news. They had found Bandoola's dead body.

Elephant Bill was stunned. He asked the men to take him to Bandoola. Elephant Bill was moved to tears when he saw him. His friend of more than 20 years was gone.

Williams took control of his emotions and told the men to stand guard over Bandoola's body. Bandoola was buried on the border of Burma and India. He carved these words into a nearby teak tree: BANDOOLA BORN 1897, KILLED IN ACTION 1944.

James Howard Williams

Elephant Bill returned to England with his family in February 1946, six months after the war ended. But he deeply missed his old friend, Bandoola. For his war deeds, Williams was given the Order of the British Empire. This special award is given to British citizens who have done a great service for Great Britain. Reporters hailed him as a hero.

Later, Williams wrote about his adventure with his elephants in Burma. One of his books was titled *Elephant Bill* and another *Bandoola*. These books were bestsellers. The legend of Elephant Bill and Bandoola lives on to this day. It was the rarest of friendships between a man and an elephant.

ELEPHANTS AT WORK TODAY

The work that Williams did with the elephants in his company has influenced the care and training of elephants ever since.

Today, thousands of elephants are still used to help haul logs in Burma. Many are born in captivity. Unfortunately, some are still taken from the wild.

The elephants drag logs through the forests to roads and rivers. From there, the logs are transported from the jungle. If lorries were used to carry the logs instead of elephants, the workers would have to build more roads through the forests. So the use of elephants helps to protect the forests from the damage that roads would cause. Elephants can also access the mountainous areas that vehicles can't reach.

Expert mahouts still care for the working elephants. The elephants are usually very well looked after. They work for five hours every day. The rest of the time they roam freely in the forest in their family groups.

When the elephants are older, they no longer have to work. They live freely in the forest. The mahouts continue to check up on them and care for them until the end of their lives.

Elephants still haul logs in Burma.

TIMELINE

15 November 1897	James Howard Williams, "Elephant Bill", is born in Cornwall. Bandoola is born the same month.
1914–18	Bill serves as a soldier during World War I.
1920	Bill starts working for the Bombay Burma Trading Corporation and moves to Burma.
c., or around, 1922	Bill meets Bandoola, who quickly becomes his favourite elephant.
1942	Bill flees Burma for India as the Japanese take the country during World War II. He returns later in the year to build bridges for the Allies with his company.
April 1944	Bill and his Elephant Company make an amazing trek from Burma to India to escape capture by the Japanese.
Late 1944	Bandoola is killed.
1945	Bill returns to England and is given the Order of the British Empire for his war deeds.
30 July 1958	Bill dies at the age of 60.

GLOSSARY

Allies group of countries that fought together in World War II; the Allies included the United States, Great Britain and France

ascent process of moving upwards

Axis Powers group of countries that fought together in World War II; the Axis powers included Japan, Italy and Germany

erode slowly wear away rock or soil, usually caused by wind, water or ice

evacuation removal of large numbers of people leaving an area during a time of danger

Gurkha soldier from Nepal in the British or Indian army

lush rich and plentiful

mahout keeper and driver of an elephant

outcroppings part of a rock layer that comes to the surface of the ground

plantation large farm where crops such as cotton and sugarcane are grown

rations soldier's daily allowance of food

recruit seek out someone for a job or team

refugee person who has to leave a place to escape war or other disasters

remote far away, isolated or distant

teak tall timber tree from southeastern Asia

terrain surface of the land

trek slow, difficult journey

ulcer sore on the skin or membrane that is often infected

vegetation all the plant life in an area

INDEX

Bombay Burma Trading Corporation 6,7

British Army 4, 8

Browne, Harold 10, 30

culture 8

elephant bridges 4, 8, 14, 54

Elephant Company, the 14, 16, 46

Hann, CW 30

India 4, 8, 14, 16, 18, 20, 56
    Burma 4, 6, 7, 8, 11, 13, 14, 18, 51, 52, 54, 56, 59, 60

mahouts 8, 10, 14, 19, 49, 61

Nepal 20

Order of the British Empire 59

refugees 20, 22, 44, 52

sandstone 28, 34, 36

Sinclair, James 52

Toke, Po 10, 11, 14, 30, 39, 40, 43, 44

White, Stanley 10, 30

World War I 4, 6

World War II 4, 7